# CELEBRITY ACTIVISTS™

# BONO

# FIGHTING WORLD HUNGER AND POVERTY

**ROSEN**
PUBLISHING®
New York

**Mary-Lane Kamberg**

*For Chad Rohrback*

Published in 2009 by The Rosen Publishing Group, Inc.
29 East 21st Street, New York, NY 10010
www.rosenpublishing.com

**Library of Congress Cataloging-in-Publication Data**

Kamberg, Mary-Lane, 1948–
Bono: fighting world hunger and poverty / Mary-Lane Kamberg.
    p. cm.—(Celebrity activists)
Includes bibliographical references (p. 103).
ISBN-13: 978-1-4042-1760-7 (library binding)
1. Bono, 1960– —Political activity—Juvenile literature. 2. Rock musicians—Biography—Juvenile literature. I. Title.
ML3930.B592K36 2007
782.42166092—dc22
[B]

2007049826

*Manufactured in Malaysia*

**On the cover:** Inset: Bono. Background: Bono is working to relieve hunger, disease, and poverty in Africa and other developing areas for children like these, who were displaced by border clashes between Chad and Sudan.

# CONTENTS

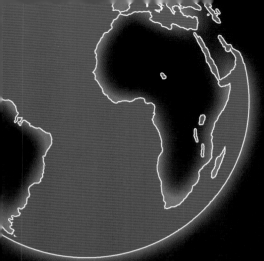

# INTRODUCTION

**W**ho do you think of when
you hear about the crisis
in Africa? For various heads
of state and world leaders in politics,
business, and religion—as well as millions
of rock and roll fans—the person can
only be Bono.

No one can argue with Bono's
success as lead singer of the band U2.
As of 2007, U2 has sold 170 million
records worldwide and won twenty-two
Grammy Awards, according to *Se7en*
magazine. But Bono is more than a
rock star. He's a man on a mission to
save a continent.

The singer uses his celebrity to
persuade the world's movers and

Bono *(center)*, lead singer of U2, uses his celebrity to call attention to the crisis in Africa and to gain access to world leaders who can make a difference. Also pictured are U2 members The Edge *(left)* and Adam Clayton.

shakers, as well as ordinary citizens, to do what they can to rescue African nations from hunger, disease, and poverty. Some of his work raises money for charity. The rest is aimed at economic development so that Africans can compete in global markets and improve their lives.

Bono was born Paul Hewson to a working-class family in Dublin, Ireland, on May 10, 1960. His father, who worked for the postal service, was a good singer himself. "My father played opera all the time," Bono says in *Bono in Conversation*. "He played it really loud. This working-class man used to stand in front of the speakers with my mother's knitting needles. Conducting, yeah. And we kids would be saying, 'Turn that down!'"

Bono's mother died of a brain aneurysm when he was fourteen. The loss left his father to rear Bono and his older brother, Norman. For a while, the three had a combative relationship, and Bono became an argumentative, rebellious teenager.

About a year after his mother's death, Bono and some other boys who hung out together and shared discontent with their suburban lives formed a performance group called Lypton Village. The group included David Howell Evans, now known to U2 fans as guitarist The Edge. One of Lypton Village's rituals was to bestow a nickname on each member.

The name "Bono" is a shortened version of the original "Bono Vox" nickname the singer got from Lypton Village. It roughly translates to "good voice" in Latin. For a while, Bono thought he'd call himself Paul Vox. Instead, he later dropped the "Vox"—and the "Paul"—and Paul Hewson became Bono.

## A Different Type of Band

In 1976, drummer Larry Mullen Jr. posted a notice at the Mount Temple Comprehensive School in Dublin, the liberal, nondenominational school Bono attended:

### DRUMMER SEEKS MUSICIANS
### TO FORM BAND

"I just thought of it as a group of people coming together to have a bit of fun," Mullen says in *U2 by U2*. "It was never anything else. No ideas. No expectations."

Bono answered the ad. So did The Edge and bassist Adam Clayton. On September 26, 1976, they met in Mullen's kitchen. The aspiring musicians could barely play instruments. In fact, The Edge had a homemade guitar. None of them wanted to sing, but Bono sang in the school choir, so he accepted the role. He had a dominant stage presence. His poetic side—and likely his early introduction to opera—made him a gifted songwriter. The chemistry among the band members was instantaneous.

From the start, U2 was a band that made a difference. In the late 1970s, punk rock was just building steam as an antisocial genre of fast music with rebellious lyrics. U2 created a different image. Although early reports in the music media called them post-punk, in reality, they defied definition. At different points during their career, they could be described as Christian, folk, pop, and rock protest, with a little blues and gospel thrown in for good measure. The variety of their music made them a unique group.

With Bono always willing to look foolish, the band projected an "uncool" image. They exposed their insecurity. But their songs, which often had spiritual or political meanings, actually communicated with the audience. Fans loved it.

U2 released their first album, *Boy*, and played the National Stadium in Dublin in 1980. In the beginning, the band gained popularity only in Europe. But the second album, *October*, released the following year, got play time across "the Pond" (the Atlantic Ocean)

In U2's early years, Bono became known for connecting with his audience— both physically and spiritually. The band's songs were known for socially conscious and religious lyrics.

on alternative rock stations on college campuses in the United States. Two more albums followed in 1983, as U2 gained fame and popularity.

In 1984, the always socially conscious band joined other rock stars to record the song "Do They Know It's Christmas?" under the name Band Aid. The single was a fund-raiser for famine relief in Ethiopia. The money raised by Band Aid bought food and supplies, but distribution was a challenge. Organizers needed a fleet of trucks.

The idea of a fund-raising concert was born; U2 joined in with other recording artists to do their part.

A worldwide television audience of more than 1.5 billion saw the 1985 Live Aid concert, which raised $245 million for famine relief in Ethiopia. After the concert, Bono traveled to Africa to see the crisis for himself.

# A Leap of Faith

With separate broadcasts from London and Philadelphia, as well as performances from Japan, Australia, Holland, Yugoslavia, Russia, and Germany, Live Aid was the biggest live rock event in history. According to BBC News, more than 1.5 billion people worldwide watched sixteen hours of live music by twenty-two acts in Wembley Stadium in London and thirty-six acts in JFK Stadium in Philadelphia. In all, with a goal of only $1.64 million, the concert raised $245 million, according to www.BobGeldof.info, the official site of Bob Geldof, the Boomtown Rats singer who organized both Band Aid and Live Aid.

The concert was U2's first worldwide exposure. They had seventeen minutes to perform, and they planned to play several songs, including their then-current hit, "Pride." But Bono spoiled the performance—or so the other band members thought. They were playing a song called "Bad," when Bono, in a move later called "the Leap," jumped off the stage and danced with a woman he pulled from the crowd. With their lead singer lost in the audience, the musicians kept playing, looking at each other and wondering what was going on. Bono's stunt used up the remaining time allotted. U2 left the stage without playing their hit. The other members were furious. Bono thought they might fire him. But the next day, the British press gave the band rave reviews, with a general consensus that Bono had stolen the show.

At the time, Bono couldn't know that "the Leap" was the first step in his journey as a spokesperson for Africa and human rights.

# CHAPTER ONE

## The Garden of Eden

In 1985, Bono worked as a volunteer in Ajibar, Ethiopia. The northeastern African nation is thought to be the cradle of civilization. Anthropologists agree the first humans lived there. About fifty thousand years ago, in a migration known as the Great Leap Forward, these early humans moved to populate the rest of the planet.

Once considered the Garden of Eden, the Ethiopia of 1985 suffered the ravages of civil war, drought, and famine. It was a place with severe hunger and poverty. Shortly after U2's performance at Live Aid, a representative of World Vision invited Bono to Africa to see for himself where the money he helped raise went. World Vision is a Christian humanitarian organization that received Live Aid funds. Bono and his wife, Ali, agreed to go, but without the usual celebrity publicity.

They were unprepared for what they saw at their destination, an orphanage and feeding station in the mountains. The camp was a small town made of wood and corrugated iron, surrounded by barbed wire. The barbed wire kept out those the volunteers couldn't feed because there was not enough food. Bono and Ali were horrified by the living conditions.

"It's a truly shocking sight," Bono says in *U2 by U2*, "to wake up and look over a hill, the morning mist hanging, and see thousands and thousands of people in rags who've walked all night to come to our feeding station."

During the three weeks they spent there, Bono and Ali helped develop educational programs. They worked with a nurse to write a one-act play about safe childbirth. And Bono wrote a song to teach hungry children not to eat the seeds needed to plant the next year's crops. Their work was translated into Amharic, the language of the people there.

In Ethiopia, Bono worked at an orphanage and feeding station taking care of adults and children who were malnourished due to severe drought and famine. While there, he wrote songs to teach children not to eat seeds intended for the following year's crop.

Bono taught the song to the children. The youngsters sang it throughout the camp and taught it to their parents.

Before Bono left the orphanage, an Ethiopian man approached with his son. To the man, the rock star was just another volunteer. In fact, with no electricity or home, let alone a television, it was unlikely the man knew what a rock star was. The man focused instead on daily needs of food, shelter, and drinking water. In a conversation Bono later related in *U2 by U2*, the man asked where Bono was from.

"Ireland," Bono said.

"You can afford to take this boy. You can look after this boy."

"I can't," Bono said. "I can't take him with me."

"Then he will surely die."

Bono never learned what happened to the boy. He says in *U2 by U2*, "In a certain sense I have always taken that boy with me, and if the rage rises up inside me, as sometimes it does, it's usually him I'm thinking of."

## Hunger and Starvation

In Ethiopia, Bono learned more about the trouble Africa faces. Without the basic needs of food, health care, water, sanitation, and education, people experience hunger and disease that lead to early death. Africans have the lowest life expectancy in the world. Life expectancy reflects the overall health of a country. According to statistics reported on About.com: Geography, three African countries are

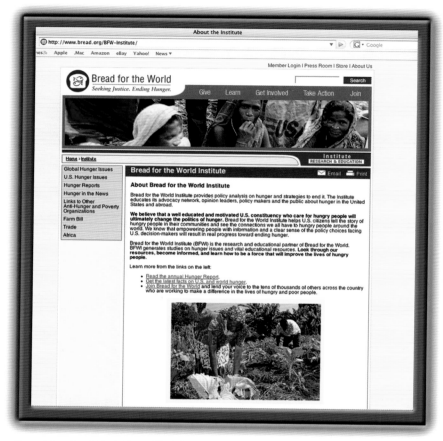

Bread for the World is a Christian organization that lobbies members of the U.S. Congress on behalf of those suffering from hunger throughout the world. It is a partner in the ONE Campaign, which Bono helped start.

at the bottom of the list. In Swaziland, life expectancy is 33.2 years, in Botswana it is 33.9 years, and in Lesotho it is 34.5 years. By comparison, the life expectancy for Americans is 77.7 years.

Today, people living in poverty in Africa drastically outnumber the poor in the United States. According to the U.S. Census Bureau, in 2006 approximately 36.5 million people in the United States were officially considered poor. That represents 12.3 percent of the population. In Africa, on the other hand, a nongovernmental organization (NGO) called Bread for the World estimates 80 percent of the African population of 700 million must try to survive on less than $2 a day.

Hunger is one of the serious results of this poverty. According to Bread for the World, one-third of the African population is malnourished. And the ONE Campaign to Make Poverty History, an advocacy NGO Bono helped found, says that every day, 200 million Africans go without food. They can't produce enough to feed themselves, and they can't afford to buy it.

## HIV and AIDS

Another consequence of poverty is disease. Poor countries often lack prevention programs, health-care facilities, trained health-care workers, technology, and medicine. According to ONE, African countries

World Vision, another ONE Campaign partner, sends doctors and relief workers to Africa to fight such diseases as AIDS, tuberculosis, and malaria through treatment and prevention programs.

have the world's highest incidence of infection with human immunodeficiency virus (HIV), the virus that causes acquired immunodeficiency syndrome (AIDS).

In the African nations of Botswana, Namibia, Swaziland, and Zimbabwe, an estimated 20 to 26 percent of people between the ages of fifteen and forty-nine are either HIV positive or have full-blown AIDS. In nine other African countries south of the

Sahara Desert, approximately 10 percent of the adult population is infected.

Worse, revealed the Food and Agricultural Organization of the United Nations, Africa accounts for only 10 percent of the world's population, but 90 percent of new cases of HIV infection and 83 percent of the world's AIDS deaths are found there. According to ONE, AIDS killed 2.1 million Africans in 2006. The death toll threatens an entire generation of teachers, health-care workers, and farmers needed to run communities and teach children the skills they'll need in the future.

Many of those who die from AIDS leave behind orphans that an already poor community must support. A report compiled by the United Nations Children's Emergency Fund, UNAIDS, and the U.S. President's Emergency Plan for AIDS Relief says that twelve million children in sub-Saharan Africa have lost one or both parents to AIDS.

## Tuberculosis and Malaria

AIDS isn't the only illness plaguing Africans. People infected with HIV are particularly susceptible to death from tuberculosis (TB), a respiratory illness spread by coughing and sneezing. According to the Reuters Foundation AlertNet, which alerts humanitarian organizations to emergencies, 250,000 new TB cases are diagnosed annually in South Africa. Tuberculosis is a curable disease. But in Africa, only 53 percent of those who get it are cured. In 2006 alone, ONE says, 550,000 people died from TB in Africa.

Public health services, with help from international health organizations, try to provide the six-month course of medication to infected Africans. But, health-care delivery systems are primitive and ill-equipped. Often, patients get only some of the medicine they need over the six-month treatment period, either because they fail to return to health clinics for the rest of their medicine, or the health clinics run out of drugs. This partial treatment strengthens the bacterium that causes TB and makes it resistant to the drugs. Officials from the World Health Organization (WHO) are concerned about an outbreak of "extremely drug-resistant tuberculosis" (XDR-TB) in South Africa. According to WHO, seventy-four of the seventy-eight African patients confirmed in 2006 to have XDR-TB died.

## Are the Numbers Reliable?

Questions about the accuracy of statistics about HIV and AIDS in Africa have arisen since the first deaths were reported. Problems include the difficulty of diagnosing the illness and determining the cause of death, not to mention trouble reporting the numbers.

Along with other health-care challenges, African health clinics often can't perform double-confirmation studies to accurately determine the presence of HIV. The technology and supplies are too expensive or unavailable. And some patients don't return to the clinics to complete the diagnosis.

People with AIDS usually die from other illnesses that infect them when their immune systems fail. Some of the deaths may be attributed to pneumonia or TB. On the other hand, deaths from TB or other illness may inaccurately be recorded as death from AIDS. Therefore, estimates based on the numbers may be flawed.

Regardless of the exact numbers, however, observers agree that the health status of Africans lags well behind people in richer areas. The sad part is most of the HIV-AIDS, TB, and malaria cases are preventable, treatable, or curable with the right health-care programs, technology, and drugs.

Malaria is another disease devastating the continent. The flu-like illness caused by a parasite and spread by mosquitoes is both preventable and treatable. Yet, according to ONE, malaria annually kills one million Africans—most of them children—and costs the continent $12 million per year in lost economic growth.

## Other Poverty-Related Challenges

Additional challenges include early deaths of mothers and children and lack of clean drinking water, sanitation, and educational opportunities.

ONE says the risk of a woman in a developed country dying during childbirth is 1 in 2,800. In Africa, the chance is 1 in 20. The poor countries lack skilled health professionals, equipment, and supplies necessary for safe childbirth.

Clean water is another basic need that is not met in Africa. Water supplies contaminated with germs and lack of proper sanitation contribute to the spread of malaria and other diseases. Yet, ONE estimates 314 million people in sub-Saharan Africa don't have easy access to clean water. Women and young girls, often charged with the job of collecting water, spend many hours each day walking long distances for it.

In Africa, walking long distances in search of clean drinking water is a daily activity, usually performed by women and young girls. Providing this basic human need means girls can't attend the few schools available to them.

This task itself keeps many young girls out of school. In a study reported by ONE, girls were 12 percent more likely to go to school if clean water was closer than fifteen minutes away. But girls have another obstacle to overcome in order to get an education. With so much illness among adults in their communities, girls often must stay home to care for sick and dying relatives.

As Bono says in *Bono in Conversation*, when flying home from Ethiopia, he and Ali told each other, "We'll never forget what we've been through."

## What Causes Poverty in Africa?

Bono already knew something about the challenges facing Africa before performing in the Live Aid concert. But his trip to Ethiopia provided his first awareness that, although political corruption and natural disasters contribute to poverty in Africa, the Western world's relationships with the fifty-four countries there—particularly old debts and unfair trade policies—contribute, too.

In recent decades, corrupt political leaders diverted money sent by Western governments intended for humanitarian aid to personal and military use. As

Bono says in *Bono in Conversation*, "Corruption is probably the biggest problem facing the continent, but it is not the only one."

Other issues include old loans from rich countries to poor ones and unfair trade practices in the global marketplace. Western democratic governments, the International Monetary Fund (IMF), and the World Bank made loans to African countries during the Cold War between the United States and the Soviet Union. The loans were intended to keep African countries from becoming communist. For decades afterward—even after the leaders that made the agreements had left power—the emerging governments in those African countries were forced to spend as much as 30 percent of their annual budgets to repay those loans, according to ONE. The money countries now send to repay those loans could be better spent for clean water, sanitation, education, and health care to lift the people out of extreme poverty.

Africa is also shut out of international trade and economic development by trade practices that prevent products produced in Africa from competing in the global market. For example, U.S. farm subsidies result in commodities like cotton flooding the international

market at prices well below the amount it costs an African farmer to produce. So, African farmers cannot sell their crops for a profit.

After studying poverty in Africa, Bono realized the solution to poverty in Africa must include more than charity. The continent needs strategies to attack all causes of the situation. That's the only way Africa can move forward.

Many African farmers can't grow enough food for their families and can't afford to buy it. Where good crop yields exist, unfair trade practices prevent farmers from making a profit in global markets.

# CHAPTER TWO

## Trip to the Heartland

Bono's activism is grounded in the Scriptures. The more he studied the Bible—and the more he traveled the world witnessing wretched living conditions in developing nations—the more he asked why things are the way they are. He is particularly aware of inequality and injustice. And his faith inspires him to act. Every one of his humanitarian efforts is inspired by faith and concern for others.

As he says in *Bono in Conversation*, "You can't fix every problem. But the ones you can, you must."

On World AIDS Day in 2002, Bono was doing just that. He spoke in the pulpit at St. Paul United Methodist

Church in Lincoln, Nebraska, to launch a seven-day tour through the Midwestern United States to raise awareness of the AIDS crisis in Africa. He was there to challenge Christians to respond to the crisis as a way to live their faith.

The Judeo-Christian tradition of equality and justice forms the foundation of Bono's social work for the poor. "I will say this for the Judeo-Christian tradition," Bono says in *Bono in Conversation*, "we have at least written into the DNA the idea that God created every man equal, and that love is at the heart of the Universe."

Although Bono considers himself a Christian, he shies away from formal religion. With a Roman Catholic father and Protestant mother, Bono never developed a strong loyalty to either religion. And he was turned off by things some people did in the name of God, like fighting civil wars over religion or using television to preach the Gospel in order to enrich themselves. Bono also observed that some "religious" people failed to follow their faith in words and—perhaps more important—deeds.

But Bono's trip to churches in America's heartland convinced him that, in every religion, houses of

On World AIDS Day in 2002, Bono launched a seven-day tour of churches throughout the Midwest to raise awareness of the AIDS crisis in Africa.

worship contain good people. Perhaps he had been too hasty in judging "religion." Later, when the time came to demonstrate on the world stage, members of many Christian churches, as well as followers of other religions, marched for the cause.

At the end of the AIDS tour, author Steve Beard asked Bono about the relationship between his faith and activism on behalf of the world's poor. Bono answered in *Spiritual Journeys*, "There are 2,103 verses of Scripture pertaining to the poor. Jesus Christ only speaks of judgment once. It is not all about the things that the Church bangs on about. It's not about sexual immorality, and it is not about megalomania, or vanity. It is about the poor. 'I was naked and you clothed me. I was a stranger and you let me in.' This is at the heart of the Gospel."

## Explaining the Faith

"I think I know what God is," Bono says in *Bono in Conversation*. "God is love, and as much as I respond in allowing myself to be transformed by that love and acting in that love, that's my religion."

Bono's take on religion comes in part from serious study of Scripture. In 1981, during the early days of U2, Bono, Mullen, and The Edge became involved with the Shalom Fellowship. The charismatic, evangelical Christian group's purpose was in-depth Bible study. The attitude of the fellowship mirrored the open view of Christianity Bono encountered at his progressive school. He became a Christian and tried to live according to the Bible's teachings.

"I nearly became a full-time, not a part-time activist at that point," Bono says in *Bono in Conversation*. "At that point, we were angry. We were agitated by the inequalities in the world."

Shalom appealed to Bono's questioning nature, as well as his rebellious youth. Author Steve Stockman in *Walk On* says, "In any other city, Bono would

## The Influence of the Rock Protest

In the 1960s in America, music—specifically folk, pop, and rock and roll—became an avenue for America's youth to vent their anger and frustration over the war in Vietnam. As Bono says in *U2— The Best of Propaganda*, "I've been very inspired by the 1960s protest movements in America. Drugs may have diluted that movement, but their music played an important part in ending the Vietnam War."

Shortly after Live Aid, U2 became more political as a way of living their faith. Bono was clearly influenced by the likes of folk singer Woody Guthrie, singer/songwriter/poet Bob Dylan, the Beatles' John Lennon, and the Boomtown Rats' Bob Geldof. Bono felt particularly drawn to Lennon's wish that music be used to change the world.

The Beatles' John Lennon and other rock protest singers inspired Bono to use his own music and celebrity to reach people who could help solve problems of hunger, disease, and poverty in Africa.

> Some observers at the time thought Bono had left spiritual issues behind in favor of political ones. But Bono saw it differently. In *Walk On*, he says, "To me faith in Jesus Christ that is not aligned to social justice—that is not aligned with the poor—it's nothing."

have laughed at such middle-class, religious behavior. But in Dublin, this was radical stuff. To take Jesus seriously was far out."

In those times, reading Bibles in the back of the tour bus was more unusual than doing drugs. Having an intense spiritual faith put Bono in the minority. In the rock culture, following Jesus was a radical idea.

Another radical idea that emerged from Bono's study of Scripture was surrendering one's ego to God. This idea caused conflict—both internal conflict within Bono himself and outward conflict among the band members. Was rock stardom the place to surrender one's ego to the Lord? Was rock and roll compatible with faith? Should they leave the music business in favor of more faithful activism? Bono, The

Edge, and Mullen discussed the question for weeks. Leaders in the Shalom Fellowship pressured them to leave rock and roll and their stardom behind. The band members felt torn between the Lord and the "real" world and considered breaking up the band; maybe they should just get out in the world, where there was much to do and people to help.

"Then we came to a realization," Bono says in *Bono in Conversation*. "Where are these gifts coming from? This is how we worship God."

In the end, the band decided to continue with their music and use their fame to right some wrongs.

## Religion and Activism

For Bono, being a Christian means feeling anger at the injustice of children dying of hunger on a planet that grows enough food for everyone, mothers dying during childbirth in a world with medical knowledge and technology, and fathers dying of a diseases like AIDS or TB in a world that has a means to prevent or cure them. And being a Christian means doing something about these kinds of injustice.

In *Spiritual Journeys*, Bono says, "The Jesus Christ I believe in was the man who turned over the tables in the temple and threw the moneychangers out . . . There is a radical side to Christianity that I am attracted to. And I think without a commitment to social justice, it is empty."

For Bono, acting in God's love means working to help the poor as a way to contribute to God's kingdom on Earth. Bono doesn't want poor people to wait for justice until they go to heaven. He wants to achieve change in this life. He wants to show God's love to those living in despair and act in God's love to solve the problems that arise from poverty.

As Bono told students at Wheaton College near Chicago during the AIDS awareness tour, "'Love your neighbor' is not advice. It is a command."

## An Imperfect Faith

When U2 released its song "I Still Haven't Found What I'm Looking For" in 1987, Christian fans questioned Bono's faith. The song admitted to spiritual doubts and weakness. Would a Christian who had accepted Jesus need to continue to search? In *Walk On*, Bono calls the song "a gospel song for a restless spirit." The lyrics indicate the struggle a Christian faces *after* he or she finds Jesus.

Bono was willing to show fans that following Christ in the real world is no easy task. And being a Christian doesn't necessarily mean you have no further questions.

"At one time, I thought you had to have all the answers if you were going to write a song," Bono says in *Walk On*. "It was embarrassing to make a record that was filled with doubts and questions. . . . I realize now it's OK to say you still haven't found what you're looking for."

Despite the reaction from some Christians, the song spoke to other fans. The record hit the top of the charts, and *Rolling Stone* magazine ranked it eighth on its list of the best singles of all time.

# CHAPTER THREE

## Early Political Activism

B ono grew up during a time of political turmoil and terrorism in Northern Ireland, about an hour's drive from his home. The period, known as "The Troubles" (1968–1998), was a time of bloody civil war between Irish Catholics and British Protestants. More than 3,600 people were killed and more than 30,000 were injured, according to the CAIN Web Service based at the University of Ulster. In *Bono in Conversation*, Bono describes his childhood as a time of "a low, but significant level of violence" in Ireland.

The conflict concerned the Protestant British government's territorial claim to

the six predominantly Roman Catholic counties of Northern Ireland. With Bono's father a Roman Catholic and his mother a Protestant, the politics of the day lived under the family's roof. From U2's beginning, Bono and the band incorporated spiritual and political issues into their music. In the early 1980s, Bono denounced the violent tactics of the Irish Republican Army (IRA), which claimed responsibility for car bombings and other acts of terrorism. Although he agreed with the Irish grievances, he was against using violence to correct them.

U2 also took stands in civil wars in El Salvador and

Bono knows firsthand what it's like to live with social unrest and violence such as that in parts of Africa today. He grew up in Ireland during a Catholic-Protestant civil war known as "The Troubles."

Nicaragua. Bono visited both countries during their wars, and he voiced opposition to American foreign policy in Latin America.

The band supported a number of celebrity causes by contributing songs and talent for recordings and tribute albums, including "Do They Know It's Christmas?" (Band Aid for famine relief in Ethiopia), "What's Goin' On" (Artists Against AIDS for the United Way's September 11th Fund and the AIDS relief effort), "The Sweetest Thing" (for the Chernobyl Children's Project International), and "Miss Sarajevo" (for NetAid and War Child).

The band also participated in fund-raising concerts. In the mid-1980s, they played the Self Aid for Ireland concert to raise money and jobs for unemployed Irish citizens. In June 1986, the band was among a variety of artists and bands that played six concerts in twelve days, a tour called A Conspiracy of Hope. The tour celebrated the twenty-fifth anniversary of Amnesty International in the United States, an organization dedicated to the release of "prisoners of conscience" around the world. According to www.@U2.com, the tour raised $3 million for the organization, as well as built American awareness of the organization.

Bono and U2 have championed such political causes as Greenpeace (to encourage environmental protection), Artists Against Apartheid in South Africa (to end apartheid), War Child International (to help children affected by war), NetAid (to promote United Nations efforts to erase world poverty), the Free Burma Coalition, and others.

## Compassion Fatigue?

Although Bono was involved in a number of political and social issues, it seemed to some that he had forgotten about Africa. However, during that time, he stayed involved in a private way, without involving the other members of U2. Bono saw no plan to solve Africa's enormous problems. After all, what could he do? The need there was just too great to be solved with money raised through concerts and fund-raising recordings.

"I didn't want to be a bleeding heart without a strategy," Bono says in *Bono in Conversation*. He wanted to use his energy to attack the causes of

## Forgiving Debt

In the twentieth century, the idea of canceling debts owed to one country by another first applied to Germany. After World War II, the defeated nation could not repay loans for reconstruction. On February 27, 1953, the London Debt Agreement cut Germany's debt of thirty billion deutsche marks in half, according to the Jubilee Debt Campaign. The agreement also gave Germany easier repayment terms on the remaining fifteen billion marks.

Indonesia got a similar deal in the 1970s, when the country was allowed to wait as long as eight years to make loan payments. However, in 1982, when Mexico said it couldn't repay its loans, creditors

The standard of living in Mexico fell when creditors refused to forgive old debts. At the same time, the prices that Mexicans could get for their products on the world market stayed low.

refused to forgive the debt. Instead, they simply rescheduled the payment plan. Interest rates stayed high. The prices Mexico could get for its products in the global economy were low. The Mexican economy and standard of living fell.

Largely due to compounding interest on the old loans, debts owed by developing countries doubled between 1980 and 1990, according to the Jubilee Debt Campaign. Five years later, the total rose another 50 percent. In the United Kingdom, forty volunteer agencies formed the Debt Crisis Network in the early 1980s to lobby for debt cancellation. This early work laid the foundation for later Drop the Debt efforts around the world.

poverty, rather than simply relieving the symptoms of the problems.

At the time, Bono says in *Bono in Conversation*, "Every sort of 'Right On' movement was outside our door and knocking. We couldn't let every serious issue in. We continued our work with Amnesty International and Greenpeace."

Some wondered if Bono had "compassion fatigue." But in *Bono in Conversation*, he denies it. "I don't think we had it," he said, "but it could have been an issue for our audience if we were to take on Africa at that period. I was reading about Africa in the newspaper . . . but I wasn't anxious to stare at it for too long. But I hadn't heard any new ideas at that point."

At least not until he heard one more knock at the door.

## A New Beginning

In 1997, representatives from the Jubilee 2000 coalition came calling, and they had a plan.

The Jubilee 2000 Campaign was a grassroots movement that began in October 1997 and included more than ninety NGOs, churches, and trade unions. The organization wanted to celebrate the 2000 millennium by getting the World Bank, IMF, and Western governments to forgive the $376 billion owed to them by fifty-two of the world's poorest nations—many of them in Africa. The plan followed the 1996 Heavily Indebted Poor Countries (HIPC) initiative by the World Bank and the IMF. HIPC offered debt relief to poor countries for money owed to the world's richest countries. It was the first time that Third World debt was considered as a whole, rather than country by country. However, critics said the relief was too small, and conditions tied to reducing debts made qualifying for debt cancellation difficult.

The Jubilee 2000 Campaign spent most of its efforts educating the public about the obstacles debt placed in the way of improving living conditions of the poor. According to *U2—The Best of Propaganda*, African nations were spending $200 million a week servicing their debt to the West. And industrialized nations continued to send financial aid to the poorest countries. However, for every dollar sent in aid, the poorer nations paid nine dollars toward old loans. If the governments could spend the loan payment money in their own countries instead, they could start working their way out of poverty.

But, shouldn't those who borrow money pay it back as agreed? Usually, yes. In these cases, however, most of the debt comes from loans made in the 1970s to governments that no longer exist. In Zaire (now the Democratic Republic of the Congo), for example, President Joseph D. Mobutu ruled for more than thirty years. During Mobutu's rule, Bono said in

Africans are still paying loans made to governments that no longer exist, like the one in Zaire led by Joseph D. Mobutu, who put development money into his own bank account.

his Harvard Class Day speech in 2001, the leader sent billions of dollars he'd accept on behalf of his country into his personal Swiss bank account. Mobutu no longer reigns in Zaire, but the people who live there are still repaying the debts of the last generation. And because the loan money was squandered, those who are paying off the loans receive no benefit from the money.

For Bono, getting rich countries to drop the debt of poor ones was a question of justice, not charity. "Holding children to ransom for the debts of their grandparents, that's a justice issue," he says *in Bono in Conversation*.

Other African countries were also dealing with old debts. Tanzania and Zambia, for example, were spending two dollars to repay debt for every one dollar spent on health and education, Bono says in *Bono in Conversation*. If they could use the loan payment money on health and education instead, they could make great strides toward eradicating extreme poverty.

According to JubileeDebtCampaign.org, on May 16, 1998, seventy thousand demonstrators from Europe, Africa, Latin American, and Asia formed a human chain around the site of the annual meeting of the Group of Seven (G7). The G7 is comprised of the finance ministers and central bank governors from Canada, France, Germany, Italy, Japan, the United Kingdom, and the United States—the world's largest industrialized democracies. Combined, workers in these nations create about two-thirds of the global economic output, according to the U.S. State Department's Bureau of International Information Programs. The G7 was formed in 1975, after the global oil crisis of 1973. It meets several times a year, often with representatives from Russia in attendance, to discuss economic policy.

Protesters wanted to call the ministers' attention to the idea of canceling Third World debt as a way to end poverty. Jubilee 2000's goal was to get rich nations to forgive all developing nations' debt by New Year's Eve 1999—to celebrate the year 2000 millennium. The demonstration got the attention of Tony Blair, then the prime minister of England. Blair later met with Jubilee 2000 leaders. The campaign was gaining momentum in Britain and the rest of Europe, but organizers needed a celebrity spokesperson to be their voice in America. The thinking was if the United States went along, other nations would follow. If not, European countries that had already signed on might drop out.

That's where U2 came in.

"When we first heard about the Jubilee 2000 campaign, we were all on board," bassist Adam Clayton says in *U2 by U2*. "We recognized that this was something worth fighting for. We sat down and talked about what we could do as a band, but it quickly became apparent that it was a job for one person, and the best man for the job was Bono."

Bono accepted the challenge to represent people who have no power and no vote in the West, but whose lives are affected by decisions made by Western leaders. He talks about accepting the

## Why Africa?

Bono's interest in Africa comes in part from Ireland's connection with the continent. Irish priests and nuns supported Catholic missions there. And in the mid-1980s, many Irish felt a connection to the famine in Ethiopia because of the Irish Potato Famine of 1845, when a potato blight killed hundreds of thousands.

"Being Irish, I wasn't exposed to Africa as a cultural force, more as a moral dilemma," Bono says in *Bono in Conversation*.

For Bono, though, the key was that, in parts of Africa, money could solve problems. He took a practical approach. Regardless of the causes of poverty in Africa, money—by itself—can end hunger, treat disease, and build schools.

"There's a lot going on in Africa," Bono says in *Bono in Conversation*. "It's complex. There's corruption, there are problems of their own making, but then there are problems of our making for them, and then there are problems we could easily solve for them."

challenge in *Bono in Conversation*. "You know, celebrity is ridiculous," he says. "It's silly, but it is a kind of currency, and you have to spend it wisely. You represent a constituency that has no power, no vote, in the West, but whose lives are hugely affected by our body politic. Our clients are the people whose lives depend on these Western drugs, whose lives will be radically altered by new schools and new investment in their country. That's a position I take very seriously. They didn't ask me to represent them, Jubilee 2000 asked me to represent them, but . . . the ball kind of fell to my feet . . . and I saw a way past the goalkeeper. What am I gonna do? I'm gonna do what I can."

# CHAPTER FOUR

## The Good Voice

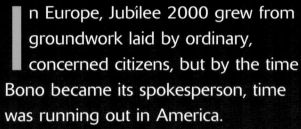

I n Europe, Jubilee 2000 grew from groundwork laid by ordinary, concerned citizens, but by the time Bono became its spokesperson, time was running out in America.

"At first I thought my job would be to engage our audience as a kind of grassroots movement to get behind this project," Bono says in *U2 by U2*. "I did some of that, but where I really came in handy was in America, working behind the scenes. Jubilee 2000 was already up and running in Europe, but in America it was not as recognized. It would be too late in 1998–1999 to grow a big enough grassroots movement. So I had to just go straight to the decision-makers and try to pitch them the ideas."

Bono first called Eunice Shriver, founder of the Special Olympics and older sister of U.S. president John F. Kennedy. She phoned her son Bobby Shriver. "Without Bobby, I could have spent years, rather than months, finding my way around Washington, D.C.," Bono says in *U2 by U2*. "Bobby Shriver had a keen sense of civic duty, a passion for social justice, and enough modesty to know when a Kennedy should attend a meeting or hide in the corridor outside."

Bono educated himself on the economics of the relationship between debt and lack of development in poor countries by meeting with top American economists. Bobby Shriver sent him to Harvard professor and noted economist Jeffrey Sachs for the ammunition he'd need to convince politicians to embrace debt relief. Sachs gave him a crash course in production, distribution, and consumption. Bono also met with Robert J. Barrow, another Harvard economics professor.

Bono set out to convince both Democratic and Republican politicians. "I wanted to get to know

Eunice Kennedy Shriver *(right)* introduced Bono to her son Bobby Shriver *(left)*. He guided the singer through the halls of the U.S. Congress to influence decision-makers on Africa's behalf.

people who might oppose the idea [of debt forgiveness]," Bono says in *Bono in Conversation*.

Shriver, a Democrat, helped Bono find someone on the Republican side of the aisle to help him. Shriver's brother-in-law Arnold Schwarzenegger introduced Bono to John Kasich, a Republican representative from Ohio's 12th District. (Kasich served in Congress for eighteen years, and his service included acting as chair of the House Budget Committee.) These two connections later helped Bono gain access to the politicians he needed to convince to support Jubilee 2000.

Bono went straight to the top. His first visit was with President Bill Clinton. They talked in a motorcade on the way to a Chicago Bears football game. In *Bono in Conversation*, the singer relates the conversation:

"[Clinton] was listening, but not intently," he says. "It was only when I asked him, did he have any good ideas for the Millennium? After all, he was going to make the big speech. Being leader of the Free World, it's a historic moment. What did he have planned? Then I noticed his concentration sharpening. 'Because,' as I explained, 'I have a really great idea.'

"I said to him: 'The dumb parade and the fanfare, is that all we're going to remember? Or could it really feel like history? Could it really be a new beginning for the people who needed a new beginning most— the poorest of the poor?' He got on that idea after a lot of questions. . . . I was saying the Millennium was the hook to hang this on. . . . It wasn't a new concept to him. What might have been new was how popular a melody it could be, that somebody like myself was interested, and that it might actually be one he could sing on New Year's Eve 1999."

## Hitting the Road

President Clinton was supportive. But not everyone in Washington would be. Bono realized that support from the president wasn't enough. Bono would have to knock on a few more doors. Bobby Shriver and John Kasich guided Bono through Congress as he met with hundreds of politicians and staffers, including ultraconservative North Carolina senator Jesse Helms. Reportedly, Helms was moved to tears by the plight of Africa's poor.

Bono's list included Pete Peterson at the Council of Foreign Relations, an independent, nonpartisan "think tank" dealing with foreign policy; David Rockefeller, founder of the Trilateral Commission, a group of private citizens from Japan, Canada, the United States, and European Union countries to foster cooperation among industrialized nations; and Larry Summers, the U.S. secretary of treasury (1999–2001), who had served as chief economist of the World Bank. Bono also met with journalists and religious groups.

"Anybody who could put obstacles in our way, we met them before they could try," Bono says in *U2 by U2*. "It is absurd, if not obscene, that celebrity is a door that such serious issues need to pass through before politicians take note. But there it is. Jubilee couldn't get into some of these offices, but I could. And I knew the idea would catch fire if it was given a chance."

## The Pope in Bono's Sunglasses

Bono's efforts weren't confined to the United States. He also traveled to Europe to meet with then British prime minister Tony Blair; Jim Wolfensohn, then president of the World Bank; Horst Koehler, chairman of the IMF (and later president of Germany); Germany's chancellor Gerhard Schroeder; and then French president Jacques Chirac.

"I'm never nervous when I go to meet heads of state," Bono says in *Bono in Conversation*. "They should be nervous, because they are the ones who'll be held accountable for the lives that their decisions will impact the most."

Pope John Paul II traded a rosary for Bono's sunglasses when the singer and a delegation of musicians, economists, and church activists met to ask the pontiff to endorse the Jubilee 2000 campaign.

As the millennium neared, Bono joined a delegation of musicians, economists, and church activists who met with Pope John Paul II one hundred days before the new year. The pope was one of the first world figures to endorse Jubilee 2000. At Bono's meeting, the pontiff agreed to ask Western world leaders to move further toward debt forgiveness.

"I appeal to all persons involved and in particular to the most powerful nations to prevent the Jubilee from passing by without decisive steps toward a definitive solution to the debt problem," Pope John Paul II said, as reported in *U2—The Best of Propaganda*. "It is the poor who pay the cost of indecision and delay."

Bono, in *U2—The Best of Propaganda*, says, "I don't know how you could turn such a man down, and I don't think U.S. President Bill Clinton wants to turn this man down, or British Prime Minister Tony Blair, or German Chancellor Gerhard Schroeder."

An interesting footnote to the meeting is a trade Bono made with the pontiff. The pope tried on Bono's blue sunglasses and wanted to keep them. In exchange, the pope gave Bono a rosary.

According to *U2—The Best of Propaganda*, after the meeting, Bono joked, "The pope's run off with my sunglasses!"

Bono addressed the United Nations General Assembly in September 1999. "In the 80s, I was a proud part of the spoiled generation who brought you Live Aid, Band Aid, *We Are the World*, all that stuff," Bono said in his speech, reprinted in *U2—The Best of Propaganda*. "It was an amazing thing, that moment in time when Bob Geldof . . . led a bunch of pop stars to raise $200 million for famine relief in Africa. I was so proud of it . . . Then I learned that Africa spends $200 million every week servicing its debt to the West. It's time now to write off the un-payable debt of the world's poorest nations . . . This is 'economic slavery' whose abolition we are now talking about. Potentially, this is a fresh start for a billion people. Now that's a reason to party and a real reason to celebrate New Year's Eve '99."

Bono's UN speech coincided with the launch of NetAid, an educational project concerning global poverty aimed at the world's youth. Supporters of

## What Is NetAid?

NetAid refers both to a rock concert held October 9, 1999, and an ongoing partnership that uses the Internet to fight global poverty. The concert was webcast from venues in Geneva, London, and New York linked by satellite. Bono appeared on the London stage. The purpose of the concert was to call attention to needs in Sudan, Kosovo, and East Timor, and to raise money through online donations. According to NetAid.org, the concert reached viewers in 132 nations and raised $20 million.

In September 1999, Bono spoke at the launch of the NetAid Web site. The site helps people learn about global poverty and offers ways donors can contribute time or money to the cause.

NetAid is a public-private partnership between the United Nations Development Programme and Cisco Systems, which underwrote the concert. NetAid programs seek to teach young people about global poverty and the need for economic development. The program also offers ways young people can act through its NetAid Global Citizen Corps, NetAid Global Action Awards, and NetAid World Schoolhouse.

the project included U.S. president Bill Clinton, England's prime minister Tony Blair, former president of South Africa Nelson Mandela, and secretary general of the United Nations Kofi Annan. The following month, Bono took the stage in London as part of the awareness and fund-raising NetAid concert.

The efforts of those involved in Jubilee 2000 paid off. The United States canceled all debt owed to it by Third World countries. So did the United Kingdom, Italy, and France. And on September 18, 2000, representatives of 188 nations endorsed the United Nations' Millennium Development Goals for reducing extreme poverty by 2015. It may have seemed that Bono's work was done.

In reality, more work lay ahead.

## The United Nations' Goals for a New Millennium

On September 18, 2000, the United States was among 188 nations that proclaimed eight specific, measurable Millennium Development Goals to end extreme poverty in the world by 2015:

1. ***Eradicate extreme poverty and hunger:*** *Reduce by 50 percent the number of people living on less than a dollar a day, and reduce by half the number of people who suffer from hunger.*
2. ***Achieve universal primary education:*** *Ensure that all boys and girls complete elementary school.*
3. ***Promote gender equality and empower women:*** *Eliminate gender discrimination in primary and secondary schools by 2005 and at all educational levels by 2015.*

4. **Reduce child mortality:** *Reduce deaths of children younger than five by two-thirds.*

5. **Improve maternal health:** *Reduce by 75 percent the number of deaths of mothers during childbirth.*

6. **Combat HIV/AIDS, malaria, and other diseases:** *Stop the spread of HIV/AIDS and eliminate cases of malaria and other major diseases.*

7. **Ensure environmental sustainability:** *Blend economic development into country policies and programs; save environmental resources; bring access to safe drinking water to 50 percent of those without it; and improve the lives of at least 100 million slum dwellers by 2020.*

8. **Develop a global partnership for development:** *Develop further an open trading and financial system that addresses the special needs of the least developed countries. This includes quota-free access for exports, debt relief,*

*and development assistance, and
develop productive work for youth.*

*Source: ONE, the Campaign to Make Poverty History.*

# CHAPTER FIVE

## Doing What He Can

The international Jubilee 2000 campaign disbanded in 2001. (Debt reduction efforts later continued under Jubilee USA and the Jubilee Debt Campaign in the United Kingdom.) But Bono wasn't through.

"We had a lot of momentum going, in the United States especially," Bono says in *U2 by U2*, "and I thought it would be a mistake to let go of the extraordinary array of characters who had gathered around us. . . . We were still working on multilateral debt, which is the monies owed to the World Bank and the IMF."

And Bono was still concerned about the devastation of HIV/AIDS in Africa.

"Seven thousand Africans dying every day of a preventable, treatable disease is not a cause, it's an emergency," he says in *U2 by U2*.

Sheryl Sandberg, former chief of staff to the secretary of the treasury under President Clinton gave Bono another idea. In *U2 by U2*, she says, "A reform of trade would make an even bigger difference than a reform of the debt burden. If Africa had the same share of the global market that it had in the 1970s, it would double the amount of aid the whole world gives it in a year, every year."

With work to do, Bono, Bobby Shriver, Bob Geldof, and others from Jubilee 2000 founded an organization called DATA in Washington, D.C., and London in 2002. (DATA now has offices in Los Angeles and Berlin as well.) The "D" in DATA stands for debt. The first "A" is for AIDS. The "T" is for trade. And the second "A" is for Africa. The advocacy organization works closely with G8 leaders on the issues facing Africa. (The Group of Eight is an organization of the heads of state of the world's richest and most powerful nations: Canada, France, Germany, Italy, Japan, Russia, the United Kingdom, and the United States. They

Bob Geldof *(right)*, along with Bono and others, founded DATA in 2002. The advocacy organization that started the ONE campaign works on African issues with leaders of the world's richest and most powerful nations.

meet every year to discuss global economic and political issues.) According to DATA, its core belief is these issues are about equality and justice, not charity.

The acronym also has another meaning. "If you turn it around to focus on what the West wants for releasing funds, it also spells democracy, accountability, transparency for Africa," Bono says in *U2 by U2*.

In the United States, Bono had worked well with the Clinton administration, but by 2002, President George W. Bush was in office. Bono met with President Bush. He also brought a team from DATA to meet with then U.S. national security advisor Condoleezza Rice (later U.S. secretary of state). The group discussed ideas for development assistance. They wanted a plan that would overcome objections that much aid from the West went to building presidential palaces instead of moving a country out of poverty.

"Clearly, a lot of foreign aid had been misused in the past, propping up tinpot dictators in ways that actually did more harm than good," Bono says in *U2 by U2*.

The group developed a plan that would increase aid to countries that fought corruption and offered transparency with regard to the money they received.

President Bush, for his part, issued the Millennium Challenge in a speech about global development at the Inter-American Development Bank in Washington, D.C., in March 2002. The president created a Millennium Challenge account to fight AIDS, improve education, and use technology to improve agriculture. He doubled U.S. aid to Africa by annually adding $5 billion. According to the text of the speech published by the Office of the Press Secretary, Bush also acknowledged Bono's influence in Washington.

"Bono, I appreciate your heart," Bush said. "And to tell you what an influence you've had, Dick Cheney walked into the Oval Office. He said, 'Jesse Helms wants us to listen to Bono's ideas.'"

Bono wanted the president to include additional money to fight AIDS in Africa, and the following year, Bush did. In his State of the Union speech in 2003, he announced another $15 billion in aid over five years to fight the disease.

## Spreading the Word

Bono had learned from President Bill Clinton that more than a U.S. president's blessing was needed to achieve DATA's goals. Bono also knew the best way to speak with politicians was through their constituency. To that end, DATA began an initiative called ONE, the Campaign to Make Poverty History.

ONE is an American humanitarian organization that increases awareness of global poverty issues through educational information. It also serves as an advocacy group. It asks political leaders to live up to U.S. commitments and to address the AIDS pandemic and global poverty in a nonpartisan way. ONE lobbies on such fronts as the federal budget, presidential elections, and specific legislation relating to debt cancellation, foreign aid, and fair trade.

According to ONE.org, "ONE believes that allocating an additional 1 percent of the U.S. budget toward providing basic needs like health, education, clean water, and food would transform the futures and hopes of an entire generation in the world's poorest countries."

## What 1 Percent Can Do

An increase of international aid by approximately $29 billion will make significant progress toward reversing the effects of poverty. That amount is roughly equal to 1 percent of the 2008 U.S. federal budget of $2.9 trillion, according to the U.S. Office of Management and Budget. According to ONE, a 1 percent increase in aid will:

- Cut in half the number of people suffering from hunger
- Grant free primary education to 77 million children
- Bring clean water to 450 million people
- Bring basic sanitation to 700 million people
- Prevent deaths of 5.4 million young children from poverty-related disease
- Prevent 16,000 deaths each day from HIV/AIDS, tuberculosis, and malaria

*Source: ONE, the Campaign to Make Poverty History*

Bono promoted the ONE campaign at U2 concerts, where he appealed to the audience to take out their cell phones and text a message to join the campaign. The appeal created what Bono in *U2 by*

*U2* calls "a galaxy of diode lights." Now, cell phone lights have replaced cigarette lighters to show support at rock concerts.

According to ONE, more than 2.4 million Americans from all fifty states belonged to the organization as of July 2007. In addition, more than one hundred respected humanitarian and advocacy organizations partner with ONE. By representing so many voters, ONE's growing membership continues to get the attention of Congress, as well as other policy and decision-makers in Washington, D.C.

"ONE is becoming like the National Rifle Association in its firepower, but acts in the interest of the world's poor," Bono wrote in *Vanity Fair* magazine, where he served as guest editor of a special issue devoted to Africa.

## The Four Respects

In 2005, in an effort to stimulate trade in Africa, Bono and his wife, Ali, along with designer Rogan Gregory, founded Edun, a socially conscious, for-profit, high-fashion clothing company. Its mission statement, posted on its Web site (www.edunonline.com), is to "create beautiful clothing while fostering sustainable

In 2005, Bono, his wife, Ali *(center)*, and designer Rogan Gregory *(right)* started Edun, a clothing company that provides economic opportunities for African workers and uses organic African cotton.

employment in developing areas of the world." The clothes will be made entirely from organic African cotton and sewn by African workers.

"I want [Edun] to work as a business," Bono says in *Bono in Conversation*. "I want it to make a profit, but I also want it to contribute something to all the people in the chain."

The company works under a concept called the "four respects": respect for the place the clothes are made, respect for who makes them, respect for the materials they're made of, and respect for the consumer.

"When you buy a pair of jeans," Bono says in *Bono in Conversation*, "the story of those jeans, where the cotton was grown, who grew it, how the sewers in the factory were treated, those stories are woven into your jeans. . . . When you put on those clothes, you're going to feel better about them and yourself."

In addition, DATA is working to influence Western trade policies that keep African nations from competing in the global market. Tariffs, taxes, and agricultural subsidies that let Western farmers bring commodities to market below the cost of producing them in Africa all serve to inhibit African exports. Without equal access to the market, African nations can do little to pull themselves out of poverty.

## Recruiting the Private Sector

In 2006, Bono and Bobby Shriver started an organization called (Product) RED as a new business model.

It involves cooperation among such corporate partners as American Express, Apple, Emporio-Armani, Converse, Gap, Hallmark, and Motorola.

"To change the world we need consumer power," Bono told Alex Shoumatoff in *Vanity Fair*. "Idealists and activists alone will not get the job done. (RED) is a gateway drug into a bigger movement."

To participate, corporations divert advertising funds from existing marketing budgets to promote sales of (Product) RED–branded products. They donate a portion of the profits from sales of these products to the Global Fund for HIV/AIDS programs in Africa and around the world.

For example, Emporio-Armani offers mirrored aviator sunglasses as a (Product) RED item and donates about 40 percent of its gross profit on that item to the Global Fund, according to its Web site (www.emporioarmaniproductred.com).

Gap has an extensive line of (Product) RED clothing and accessories for men, women, and children, including a special "2 WEEKS" T-shirt. Proceeds from sales of that shirt are enough to pay for two weeks worth of an HIV patient's medicine.

Hallmark joined (Product) RED in time for the 2007 Christmas season. According to Hallmark.com, the company donates 8 percent of the net wholesale sales of a (Product) RED collection of cards with sound, note cards, holiday greeting cards, customizable photo cards, easy-to-use E-Cards, gift wrap, and artisan-made gifts.

According to JoinRed.com, the (RED) Manifesto says, "(RED) is not a charity, it is simply a business model. You buy (RED) stuff. We get the money, buy the pills and distribute them. They take the pills, stay alive, and continue to take care of

Queen Rania Al Abdullah of Jordan *(left)* and Bobby Shriver *(right)* were on hand when Hallmark unveiled its (Product) RED line of greeting cards and other products in New York City in 2007.

their families and contribute socially and economically in their communities."

## The Gleneagles Promises

Five years after the millennium, the G8 was scheduled to meet in Gleneagles, Scotland. The United Kingdom was serving as president of the European Union, and Prime Minister Tony Blair and chancellor of the Exchequer (the British government's chief financial officer) Gordon Brown were in charge of the G8 agenda. Both officials had previously supported issues of poverty in Africa. So, the time was right to influence G8 leaders to do more to fight extreme poverty.

Soon, a ten-concert series called Live 8 was born, with venues in every G8 country held between July 2 and July 6, 2005. According to live8live.com, 150 bands and 1,250 musicians participated, including U2, who sang "Sergeant Pepper's Lonely Hearts Club Band" with the Beatles' Paul McCartney. Live 8 asked not for the audience's money. It asked for its voices. The result was a worldwide lobbying effort to influence G8 leaders to do more to improve African health care and education.

**The Gleneagles Promises**

When the G8 leaders met, they agreed to the following goals, which live8live.com says can save more than four million lives a year by 2010:

- Fifty billion dollars more in aid annually by 2010
- One hundred percent debt cancellation for up to forty poor countries, with eighteen benefiting in 2005
- Primary schools for all children by 2015
- Free, quality primary education and basic health care for all children
- AIDS drugs for all who need them, and care for all AIDS orphans
- Treatment and bed nets to cut the number of deaths from malaria in half
- Vaccinations to eradicate polio
- Immunization against malaria for 85 percent of the most susceptible Africans

*Source: www.live8live.com*

According to live8live.com, an estimated three billion people watched the concerts and sent world leaders a message: Make poverty history. But would the leaders hear them?

Bono, quoted on www.live8live.com, said, "It is this movement of church people and trade unionists, soccer moms and student activists that will carry the spirit of Live 8 on. It is this movement, not rock stars, who will make it untenable in the future to break promises to the most vulnerable people on this planet. That was always why we put on the concerts."

The G8 paid attention. Leaders promised additional development assistance and forgave $40 billion in debt owed by fourteen African nations and four other countries.

# CHAPTER SIX

## Is It Working?

A year after the Gleneagles G8 meeting, the Make Poverty History Campaign was making history. Writing in the British national newspaper the *Guardian*, economics editor Larry Elliott wrote, "[British] prime minister Tony Blair and [British] financial minister Gordon Brown secured far more than had been achieved at any previous G-8 summit."

Critics said the G8 nations made a lot of noise and "pretended for a day, at least, that they really cared about the world's poor."

But, Elliott continued, "Quite a lot has changed. . . . The message for the

Tony Blair *(left)*, then the British prime minister, and Gordon Brown *(right)*, then Britain's financial minister, led G8 leaders at the 2005 meeting in Gleneagles, Scotland, to forgive $40 million in debt.

G-8 should [be] doing the right thing makes a difference."

The debt reduction that began with Jubilee 2000 paid immediate results. In 2001, Bono told Harvard students in his Class Day address, twice as many children in Uganda attended school, and one health clinic in Uganda that vaccinated children against measles nearly wiped out the disease in its district. In 1999, measles there killed hundreds of children.

The next year, health-care workers saw fewer than ten cases. In Mozambique, a 42 percent debt reduction let the government increase health-care spending by $14 million.

To qualify for debt cancellation, poor countries must reform economic policies and agree to spend debt savings to reduce poverty. In 2007, according to ONE, fourteen African countries had qualified for debt relief in return for reform. Also, eighteen African countries had qualified for 100 percent debt cancellation of nearly $2 billion in loan payments per year.

According to the Jubilee Debt Campaign, overall, the world's richest countries have cancelled more than $83 billion in loans to twenty developing countries. Money once used to make loan payments now goes to public services, with an average budget increase of 20 percent. These countries have increased health-care spending by 70 percent and education spending by 40 percent.

According to ONE, Mozambique has built schools and immunized children against tetanus, whooping cough, and diphtheria. And Cameroon used its savings to start a program for HIV/AIDS prevention.

To put pressure on Chancellor Angela Merkel in advance of the G8 summit, Bono said in a 2007 press conference that Germany had broken its promise of aid for Africa.

## Fighting Disease

Money is helping in the fight against HIV/AIDS and other death-sentence diseases in emerging nations. In 2002, 1 percent of Africans with HIV infection who needed antiretroviral drugs got them, according to *Vanity Fair* magazine. By 2007, 28 percent got treatment. More than 1.34 million people were getting needed medicine for HIV/AIDS, with

## What You Can Do

If anything, Bono has proven that one person can make a difference. If you want to help eliminate extreme poverty, then do some of the following activities assembled from the Web sites for DATA, ONE, and (Product) RED:

- Learn about the issues.
- Spread the word at your school, workplace, and place of worship.
- Sign the ONE Declaration (http://www.one.org/declare) and e-mail your friends to do the same.
- Contact your representatives in government in support of legislation that favors DATA goals (http://www.one.org/takeaction).
- Wear a white ONE wrist band or Edun T-shirt, or buy other ONE merchandise (available at http://store.one.org).
- Buy (Product) RED™ branded merchandise (http://www.joinred.com/products).
- Volunteer for ONE activities in your local area.
- Donate or raise money.

What Bono told the United Nations General Assembly in New York in 1999 still applies today. He said, "What you should do now is stay informed, write to your politicians, sign a petition, make yourself heard."

another 1,450 new individuals getting treatment every day. In one year (December 2005 to December 2006), an additional 530,000 African patients got the drugs.

In Rwanda, the first country to distribute antiretroviral drugs from the Global Fund, the percentage of citizens with HIV infection has dropped from 21 percent in the 1980s to 3 percent in 2007, according to *Vanity Fair*. Its president, Paul Kagame, established an educational "ABC" program based on abstinence, being faithful, and using condoms. Another campaign urged citizens to be tested for HIV. By 2007, more than 635,000 had been tested, and nearly 14,500 had received free antiretroviral medicine. In Zambia, the Global Fund sponsored a similar program.

Former U.S. president Bill Clinton helped make drugs for HIV treatment affordable by convincing four drug manufacturers in the United States and two in India to provide medication at a greatly reduced price. The U.S. manufacturers cut the price of one person's medicine from $10,000 per year in the West to $140 a year in Africa. Money pledged by President George W. Bush went to pay for drugs for Africans who still couldn't afford the reduced price. The Indian companies have agreed to provide advanced treatment for $1 per day to 1.5 million Africans by 2010.

With its advertising slogan, "Be a Good-Looking Samaritan," (Product) RED partners donated $25 million to the Global Fund to treat AIDS, tuberculosis, and malaria in its first nine months, Bono said in *Vanity Fair*. As of October 2007, JoinRed.org said (Product) Red donations exceeded $45 million; $30 million of that was already invested in AIDS programs in Ghana, Swaziland, and Rwanda.

According to ONE, in the Global Fund's first five years, it provided treatment for more than 1 million people with HIV/AIDS, 2.8 million with tuberculosis, and 23 million with malaria. It distributed 30 million insecticide-treated bed nets to prevent malaria. It supported 1.2 million orphans with basic care, and it voluntarily tested 9.4 million people for HIV infection.

## Trade and Education

Unfair trade restrictions still enforced by the World Trade Organization are slowly giving way to such fair trade–certified products as tea, fruit, rice, sugar, coffee, and chocolate. "Fair trade" practices give

## Recognition for Bono's Charitable Work

**1999** MTV Free Your Mind Award for his charitable work, particularly on behalf of Jubilee 2000

**2003** Nominated for the Nobel Peace Prize

**2003** Knight in the Order of the Legion of Honor, awarded by French president Jacque Chirac, for "tireless social activism"

**2003** International Humanitarian Award from the America/Ireland Fund

**2004** Pablo Neruda International Presidential Medal of Honour from the Government of Chile

**2005** *Time* magazine's Person of the Year (along with Bill and Melinda Gates) as the person who most affected the world that year

**2005** Order of Liberty, awarded by Portugal's president Jorge Sampaio in recognition of the band's humanitarian efforts

**2005** Nominated for Nobel Peace Prize

**2006** Nominated for Nobel Peace Prize

**2007** Appointed an honorary Knight Commander of the Most Excellent Order of the British Empire in recognition of his services to the music industry and for his humanitarian work by Queen Elizabeth II (full knighthood is reserved for British citizens)

**2007** The National Association for the Advancement of Colored People (NAACP) Image Awards

Chairman's Award for distinguished public
service
**2007** The Philadelphia Liberty Medal, from the
National Constitution Center for advancing the
cause of liberty around the world

farmers fair compensation and encourage sustainable
farming methods. In other words, they help Africans
help themselves through economic efforts rather
than charity.

African nations are also making inroads in education. Overall, according to ONE, twenty million
sub-Saharan African children became new students
in Tanzania, Mozambique, Kenya, Malawi, Uganda,
Ethiopia, and Rwanda between 2000 and 2004.
Between 2000 and 2003, Tanzania had nearly five
million children newly enrolled in school. In Ghana
in 2005, primary school enrollments rose 14 percent.
Nigeria used its $750 million loan payment savings
from 2006 to train new teachers.

Increased access to school reaps many benefits.
ONE says if a mother goes to school for five years,

her children have a 40 percent better chance of living beyond age five. Educated mothers are 50 percent more likely to get their children immunized. And women's average income rises between 10 percent and 20 percent for each year they spend in school.

In short, even though the job of eliminating the world's extreme poverty is far from over, the efforts of so many—including Bono—make a difference in measurable ways.

So, what does the future hold? Bono seems to know.

In concert during U2's 2005 Vertigo Tour, as the first four notes of the song "Miracle Drug" sounded, Bono introduced guitarist The Edge by telling the following story, repeated in *U2 by U2*:

> *These four notes give me faith in the future. You know, Edge is from the future . . . but not just the future on this planet: he comes from a different planet.*
>
> *And in fact Larry, Adam, and I were all there when his spaceship arrived on the north side of Dublin. And the door opened and out came this strange creature.*

Larry went up to him and said, "Who are you?"

He said, "I'm The Edge."

And Adam said, "Where are you from?"

And Edge said, "I'm from the future."

And Larry said, "What's it like?"

And Edge said, "It's better."

# GLOSSARY

**AIDS**  Acquired immunodeficiency syndrome; disease caused by human immunodeficiency virus.

**Amharic**  The native language of Ethiopia.

**amnesty**  A government pardon for political offenses.

**anthropologist**  A social scientist who studies physical and cultural human development.

**antiretroviral drug**  Medication used to treat patients with HIV infection; these drugs slow reproduction of the virus in the body.

**apartheid**  A racial segregation policy with roots in the colonial period beginning in 1652; the policy was officially imposed by white minority governments in South African countries, particularly in the Republic of South Africa between 1948 and 1994 (from the Afrikaans word for "apartness").

**bono vox**  Latin term for "good voice."

**constituency**  The voters or district an elected official represents.

**G8**  The Group of Eight; heads of state of the world's richest and most powerful nations: Canada, France, Germany, Italy, Japan, Russia, the United Kingdom, and the United States; they meet every year to discuss global economic and political issues.

**grassroots movement**  A political or social movement that starts among people at the local level.

**G7**  The Group of Seven; the finance ministers and central bank governors of Canada, France, Germany, Italy, Japan, the United Kingdom, and the United States. They meet several times a year to discuss economic policy. Representatives from Russia also attend their meetings.

**HIV**  Human immunodeficiency virus; the virus that causes AIDS.

**humanitarian**  A person promoting human welfare and social reform.

**industrialized nation**  A country that has developed large-scale commercial production and distribution of goods and services.

**International Monetary Fund (IMF)**  An international organization of 185 member countries that promotes monetary cooperation and exchange stability, and provides temporary financial assistance to countries.

**life expectancy**  The average life span of a newborn in a specific region.

**lobbying**  An attempt to influence legislators in
favor of a special interest or to take a specific
action, usually in regard to proposed legislation.

**malaria**  A preventable, treatable, flu-like illness
caused by a parasite and spread by mosquitoes.

**NGO**  Nongovernmental organization, usually
humanitarian in nature.

**pandemic**  Occurring over a wide geographic area
and affecting a large number of people.

**think tank**  An organization formed for intensive
research or problem solving in strategic politics;
may also apply to researching or finding solutions
related to technology.

**tuberculosis**  A bacterial infection affecting the lungs
that is spread by coughing and sneezing.

**World Bank**  An organization consisting of two insti-
tutions (the International Bank for Reconstruction
and Development, and the International
Development Association) owned by 185 member
countries that provide financial and technical
assistance in the form of low-interest loans, interest-
free credit, and grants to developing countries.

**XDR-TB**  Extremely drug-resistant tuberculosis, a
deadly strain of the respiratory disease.

# FOR MORE INFORMATION

Africare House
440 R Street NW
Washington, DC 20001
(202) 462-3614
Web site: http://www.africare.org
An African American organization that addresses
    needs related to health and HIV/AIDS, as well
    as food security and agriculture in twenty-five
    sub-Saharan African countries.

American Red Cross National Headquarters
2025 E Street NW
Washington, DC 20006
(703) 206-8000
Web site: http://www.redcross.org
An organization that provides neutral emergency
    services to victims of war and natural disasters,
    and works to relieve suffering in countries around
    the world.

Bread for the World
50 F Street NW, Suite 500

Washington, DC 20001

(800) 82-BREAD (822-7323)

E-mail: bread@bread.org

Web site: http://www.bread.org

A Christian advocacy organization that promotes an
end to world hunger.

Canadian International Development Agency

200 Promenade du Portage

Gatineau, QB K1A 0G4

Canada

(800) 230-6349

E-mail: info@acdi-cida.gc.ca

Web site: http://www.acdi-cida.gc.ca

The leading Canadian agency for developmental
assistance, this organization also responds to food
and agricultural needs in Ethiopia, Eritrea, Kenya,
Somalia, and Uganda.

International Medical Corps

1919 Santa Monica Boulevard, Suite 400

Santa Monica, CA 90404

Web site: http://www.imcworldwide.org

A humanitarian medical organization that sponsors
   health-care training, and relief and development
   programs.

Partnership Africa Canada (PAC)
323 Chapel Street
Ottawa, ON K1N 7Z2
Canada
(613) 237-6768
E-mail: info@pacweb.org
Web site: http:/www.pacweb.org
Focuses on policy matters pertaining to sustainable
   human development in Africa.

World Vision
P.O. Box 9716, Dept. W
Federal Way, WA 98063-9716
(888) 511-6548
E-mail: info@worldvision.org
Web site: http://www.worldvision.org
A Christian relief and development organization
   seeking to "end poverty, fight hunger, and
   transform lives."

# Web Sites

Due to the changing nature of Internet links, Rosen Publishing has developed an online list of Web sites related to the subject of this book. This site is updated regularly. Please use this link to access the list:

http://www.rosenlinks.com/cea/bono

# FOR FURTHER READING

Bono. *On the Move*. Nashville, TN: W Publishing Group, 2006.

Calderisi, Robert. *The Trouble with Africa: Why Foreign Aid Isn't Working*. Houndmills Basingstoke, England: Palgrave Macmillan, 2007.

French, Howard W. *A Continent for the Taking: The Tragedy and Hope of Africa*. New York, NY: Vintage, 2005.

Greene, Melissa Faye. *There Is No Me Without You: One Woman's Odyssey to Rescue Africa's Children*. New York, NY: Bloomsbury USA, 2006.

Guest, Emma. *Children of AIDS: Africa's Orphan Crisis*. Second edition. London, England: Pluto Press, 2003.

Lewis, Stephen. *Race Against Time: Searching for Hope in AIDS-Ravaged Africa*. Second Edition. Toronto, ON: House of Anansi Press, 2006.

Ndebele, Njabulo S., Nobantu Rasebotsa, and Meg Samuelson. *Nobody Ever Said AIDS: Poems and Stories from Southern Africa*. Roggebaai, South Africa: Kwela Books, 2007.

Nolen, Stephanie. *28: Stories of AIDS in Africa.*
New York, NY: Walker & Company, 2007.

Sachs, Jeffrey. *The End of Poverty: Economic Possibilities for Our Time.* New York, NY: Penguin 2006.

Theroux, Paul. *Dark Star Safari: Overland from Cairo to Cape Town.* Boston, MA: Mariner Books, 2004.

Winge, Kevin. *Never Give Up/Vignettes from Sub-Saharan Africa in the Age of AIDS.* Saint Paul, MN: Syren Book Company, 2006.

# BIBLIOGRAPHY

Assayas, Michka. *Bono in Conversation with Michka Assayas*. New York, NY: Riverhead Books, 2005.

@U2.com. "U2 and the Conspiracy of Hope Tour." June 1986. Retrieved October 13, 2007 (http://www.atu2.com/events/86/conspiracyofhope).

BBC History. "Northern Ireland: 'The Troubles.'" British Broadcasting Co. 2007. Retrieved August 21, 2007 (http://www.bbc.co.uk/history)/recent/troubles/the_troubles_article_01.shtml).

BBC News. "U2 Steal Grammys Glory from Carey." British Broadcasting Co. February 9, 2006. Retrieved October 2, 2007 (http://news.bbc.co.uk/nolpda/ukfs_news/hi/newsid_4692000/2692222.stm?).

Beard, Steve. *Spiritual Journeys: How Faith Has Influenced Twelve Music Icons*. Lake Mary, FL: Relevant Media Group, 2003.

BobGeldof.info. "Live Aid." Retrieved September 20, 2007 (http://www.bobgeldof.info/Charity/liveaid.html).

Bono. "Bono's Liberty Medal Acceptance Speech." September 27, 2007. Philadelphia, PA. Retrieved

October 13, 2007 (http://www.atu2.com/news/article.src?ID=4755).

Bono. "Message 2U." *Vanity Fair*, July 2007, p. 32.

"Bono: The Right Man, the Right Time." *Time*. February 26, 2002. Retrieved October 15, 2007 (http://www.time.com/time/columnist/elliott/article/0,9565,213141,00.html).

Bono. "Three Chords and the Truth" (Class Day address at Harvard University). June 6, 2001. Retrieved September 10, 2007 (http://www.everything2.com/index.pl2node_id+1211409).

Bono, The Edge, Adam Clayton, Larry Mullen Jr., with Neil McCormick. *U2 by U2*. New York, NY: HarperEntertainment, 2006.

Bush, George W. "President Proposed $5 Billion Plan to Help Developing Nations: Remarks by the President on Global Development." Delivered at the Inter-American Development Bank, Washington, D.C., Office of the Press Secretary. March 14, 2002. Retrieved October 16, 2007 (http://www.whitehouse.gov/news/releases/2002/03/20020314-7.html).

Collins, Carol. "'Break the Chains of Debt!' International Jubilee 2000 Campaign Demands

Deeper Debt Relief." *Africa Recovery Online.*
Retrieved October 12, 2007 (http://www.un.org/
ecosocdev/geninfo/afrec/subjindx/132debt2.htm).

Elliott, Larry, "Gleneagles Did Not Short-Change
Africa." *Guardian.* July 3, 2006. Retrieved
October 17, 2007 (http://www.guardian.co.uk/
debt/story/0,,1811311,00.html).

Gitzduff, Mari, and Liam O'Hagan. "The Northern
Ireland Troubles: INCORE Background Paper."
CAIN Web Service. University of Ulster.
September 25, 2007. Retrieved October 13, 2007
(http://cain.ulst.ac.uk/othelem/incorepaper.htm).

Jubilee Debt Campaign. "The Birth of Jubilee 2000."
Retrieved October 12, 2007 (http://www.
jubleedebtcampaign.org.uk/?lid=282).

Jubilee Debt Campaign. "Origins of the Debt
Movement." Retrieved October 12, 2007
(http://www.jubleedebtcampaign.org.uk/?lid-279).

Luithlen, Susanne. "Report on the Activities on
the 50th Anniversary of the London Debt
Agreement 1953." March 13, 2003. Retrieved
October 12, 2007 (http://www.erlassjahr.de/
content/languages/englisch/dokumente/
20030313_report_londonintactivities.rtf).

Malan, Rian. "AIDS in Africa: In Search of the Truth." *Rolling Stone*. November 22, 2001.

Margiasso IV, Nick. "Bono by the Numbers." *Se7en*. February 2007. Retrieved October 2, 2007 (http://www.sevenmagonline.com/articles/ bono_by_the_numbers).

Meyer Sound. "Wrap Up of the NetAid Concert." Meyer Sound News. November 1999. Retrieved October 15, 2007 (http://www.meyersound.com/ news/1999/netaid/).

NetAid. "NetAid History." Retrieved October 15, 2007 (http://www.netaid.org/about/history.html).

Rosenberg, Matt. "Life Expectancy." About.com: Geography. August 19, 2007. Retrieved September 25, 2007 (http://geography.about.com/ od/populationgeography/a/lifeexpectancy.htm).

Scharen, Christian Batalden. *One Step Closer: Why U2 Matters to Those Seeking God*. Grand Rapids, MI: Brazos Press, 2006.

Shoumatoff, Alex. "The Lazarus Effect." *Vanity Fair*. July 2007, pp. 156–161, 221–223.

Stockman, Steve. *Walk On: The Spiritual Journey of U2*. Lake Mary, FL: Relevant Media Group, 2003.

U.S. Census Bureau. "Poverty: 2006 Highlights."
Retrieved September 24, 2007 (http://www.
census.gov/hhes/www/poverty/poverty06/
pov06hi.html).

U.S. State Department. "What Is the Group of 8?"
Retrieved October 14, 2007 (http://usinfo.state.
gov/ei/economic_issues/group_of_8/what_is_
the_g8.html).

*U2, The Best of Propaganda*. New York, NY:
Thunder's Mouth Press, 2003.

# INDEX

## About the Author

Mary-Lane Kamberg is a professional writer and speaker and former chair of Writers in the Schools for the Kansas Authors Club. She frequently visits classrooms for career and creative-writing workshops. In addition to ten books and hundreds of articles for adults, she has written extensively for teens in such magazines as *Current Health, Current Consumer and Lifestudies, Swimming World,* and *TeenAge.* While writing this book, she discovered U2 is her son-in-law's favorite band and that he held Bono's cue cards when the singer was filming a public service announcement in Chicago. She has signed on to the ONE Declaration and often wears her INSPI(RED) T-shirt from the Gap.

## Photo Credits

Cover, cover (inset), p. 1 (inset), pp. 1, 5, 9, 10–11, 32, 40–41, 44, 69, 75, 78–79 © Getty Images; pp. 16, 28–29, 62, 84 © AP Photos; p. 20 © Kevin Fleming/Corbis; pp. 25, 55, 86 © AFP/Getty Images; p. 34 © Michael Ochs Archive/Getty Images; p. 48 © Time-Life Pictures/Getty Images; p. 59 © Reuters/Corbis.

Designer: Tahara Anderson; Editor: Bethany Bryan
Photo Researcher: Marty Levick